GLOW

Establish boundaries, build confidence
& attract healthy relationships

Janessa M. Borges, LCSW

GLOW: Establish boundaries, build confidence & attract healthy relationships

Copyright © 2025 Janessa Borges

All rights reserved. No part of this book may be reproduced, stored in a retrieval system, or transmitted in any form or by any means— electronic, mechanical, photocopying, recording, or otherwise— without the prior written permission of the publisher, except for brief quotations in reviews or articles.

This book is a work of nonfiction intended for informational and educational purposes only. While the author is a licensed therapist, this book does not establish a therapist-client relationship, nor does it serve as a substitute for professional mental health care, diagnosis, or treatment. If you are experiencing distress or require professional support, please seek the guidance of a qualified mental health provider. The author and publisher disclaim any liability for the use or misuse of the information presented herein.

Published by Latinas Empowering Latinas LLC
Naples, FL
https://www.janessaborges.com/

ISBN: 979-8-9926530-9-0

Cover Design by Janessa Borges
Interior Layout by Janessa Borges

Printed in the United States of America

First Edition: 2025

For permissions, bulk purchases, or media inquiries, contact: janessamborges@gmail.com

Table of Contents

INTRODUCTION	1
EXERCISES	3
ABOUT ME	5
CLARITY	7
REFLECT	13
DIG DEEP	19
BREAKING DOWN WALLS	25
CREATING HEALTHY BOUNDARIES	27
FEAR VS. CHANGE	31
ARE YOU YOUR OWN WORST ENEMY?	35
MASKS	39
PURGE	47
COMPROMISE VS. SACRIFICE	53
THE LIGHTHOUSE BEACON	57
SPRING CLEANING	63
COMMUNICATION	66
BE TRUE TO YOURSELF	72
BE KIND TO YOURSELF	80
SELF-CARE	88
OVERCOMING YOUR BIGGEST FEARS	92
OVERCOMING PERFECTIONISM	96
RESTRUCTURE YOUR LIFE	102

CREATING YOUR UTOPIA	106
MAINTAINING YOUR LIFE	112
MAINTAINING YOUR LIFE EXERCISE	115

Introduction

I'm so happy you're here because I'm a huge believer that in moments like this, when you take a leap of faith that you're exactly where you need to be. My mission in life is to encourage others, especially women and particularly moms and Latinas to know they are worthy of being loved, respected and successful, and deserve to live a life they love. I'm assuming if you're here, you're not in that place quite yet, but I'm fully confident that if you focus on these lessons, do all the work without rushing, take the time you need to reflect and most importantly, make the changes you need to make in your life, you can create a life you love. Let's do this!

Give yourself tons of patience and grace.

Exercises

I created these exercises based on 21 years of working with other women that needed to make beautiful changes in their lives.

Each exercise is developed with the intention of being thoughtful, alongside soul digging inspiration to reflect and take action that will probably be scary but much needed for you to truly shine, shimmer & glow.

Always remember you are not alone on this journey.

With so much love,
Janessa

About Me

I come from a big beautiful brave Cuban family. I was born and raised in Miami to immigrants from Cuba who sacrificed their lives for their families. They taught my brother and me to be grateful, strong, respectful, loyal, and brave. And most importantly, they taught us that we can do or be anything we wanted if we put our minds and hearts into our choices. My degrees are in psychology, criminal justice, and social work. My clinical experience and graduate degree are from NYU, right smack in the middle of New York's beautiful melting pot, Greenwich Village. I graduated with honors from high school and college and I received academic and community service scholarships from all my universities. I have been in the mental health field for over 21 years and I established my practice over 14 years ago. I'm licensed in New Jersey and in Florida as a mental health therapist, but I feel limited by my office and my license because I want to reach more people all across the world. Although you do get the benefit of my experience and training as a mental health therapist in this program and these lessons, I'm not providing information as a licensed therapist and this does not constitute a doctor-patient relationship. Today and for the rest of our time together, I am your personal life coach and cheerleader standing in your corner. I want to share with you how I created a life I love and I'm here to help you create yours.

Clarity

Whether you're on a journey of self-care or working toward creating a life you truly love (which I wholeheartedly support), clarity is essential. But let's break it down—clarity doesn't mean having all the answers or a perfectly mapped-out plan. Instead, it's the process of getting honest with yourself about what you want and need. It's separating your voice from the expectations of others.

Psychologically, clarity is foundational for decision-making and emotional well-being. When we lack clarity, our minds can spiral into overthinking and indecision, leading to what's known as cognitive dissonance—that uneasy feeling when our actions and beliefs don't align. This disconnect can leave us feeling stuck, anxious, or even questioning our worth. On the other hand, clarity helps us align our actions with our core values, which research shows leads to greater satisfaction and purpose in life.

Here's why clarity is so important: without it, we often fall into default modes of living, making choices based on what others expect or what feels familiar, even if it doesn't fulfill us. This might look like following a career path someone else chose for us, staying in relationships that no longer serve us, or prioritizing others' needs while neglecting our own. Over time, this can erode our sense of self and leave us feeling unfulfilled or even resentful.

Clarity acts as a compass, grounding us in what matters most and guiding us toward decisions that align with who we truly are. However, it takes intentional effort. You have to pause, reflect, and ask yourself meaningful questions, like:

- What do I want my life to look like?

- What truly matters to me?

- Am I pursuing this goal for myself, or because I feel I should?

It's important to acknowledge that seeking clarity can feel uncomfortable at first. Why? Because it often requires confronting truths we've been avoiding—truths about what isn't working, where we feel unfulfilled, or even what we might need to let go of. But this discomfort is part of growth. It's a sign that you're moving closer to your authentic self.

Clarity also fosters a sense of control. Studies in psychology consistently show that having a clear sense of purpose and direction enhances resilience and reduces stress. When you're clear about what you want and why, you're less likely to be swayed by others' opinions or feel paralyzed by self-doubt. You can make confident decisions, set boundaries, and focus your energy on what truly aligns with your values.

Let's talk about worthiness for a moment because it's deeply tied to clarity. Many of us hesitate to get clear about what we want because, deep down, we struggle with feeling like we deserve it.

If you have absolutely any doubt, let me tell you: you are inherently worthy—of happiness, of success, of peace, of all the things you dream about. Worthiness isn't something you earn; it's something you own. And when you embrace your worth, clarity naturally follows because you stop settling for less than what you truly desire.

Here's the bottom line: without clarity, you're more likely to let life happen to you instead of actively shaping it. You leave room for indecision, insecurity, and even toxic influences to take hold. But when you prioritize clarity, you reclaim your power. You start making intentional choices that lead to a life you genuinely love.

Take this as your invitation to pause and reflect:

- What do you truly want in this season of your life?
- What would make you feel fulfilled, joyful, and at peace?
- And perhaps most importantly, why do these things matter to you?

Clarity isn't about having all the answers right now—it's about starting the journey of uncovering them. Trust yourself in this process, and know that you are more than capable of creating a life that feels true to who you are.

Reflect

Take a moment to reflect on your earliest memory of dreaming about your future. Before the opinions of others, before responsibilities of everyday life or expectations of socially imposed roles crept into your world — what did you imagine for yourself? What did you want to be, and what did you stand for? Think back to when you were a child, full of curiosity and possibility. Maybe it was while watching a movie or playing pretend when you first thought, this is who I want to be. That spark...that endless sense of possibility—do you remember it?

Now, move forward in time. What were your dreams in high school? In college? Or in your twenties? What did you hope your life would look like? Are you living that life now? And if not, what shifted along the way?

It's important to acknowledge how life's twists and turns, and the influence of others, have shaped your path. Our circumstances can leave an imprint, sometimes so subtle we don't even realize how much they've affected us. Maybe now, you feel some of those dreams are out of reach. You feel lost in a world of monotonous obligations, and self- sacrificing. You've lost a sense of who you were at your core when all of the choices and expectations started chipping away at you little by little, and before you even know it, you blink and you don't know who you are anymore. I know you can relate, because I've felt this way more times than I can count, and so has almost every single person that has sat on my couch.

Now…I want you to take a nice long deep breath, and challenge EVERY. SINGLE. THING. that you were told you had to do or had to be. However well meaning our friends, parents, teachers, (you name it) may be, we are a culture that allows others' opinions of us, and what "should be" to lead the lives we are living. We fold and conform to what we are shaped into over time. At times, we see it happening and fight against it. Other times we just feel so defeated we don't have the energy to fight, or we don't feel it's worth the fight, and oftentimes we don't even realize what's happening.

Let go of doubt and fear for a moment and reconnect with the excited, eager and unjaded version of yourself. Picture that three- or four-year-old version of you who dreamed of becoming a teacher, an astronaut, a basketball player, a princess or maybe even a superhero. That child who didn't know limitations—they just dreamed.

I want you to return to that space of possibility. Write your story from your heart. There's no right or wrong way to do this, and you don't have to share it with anyone. This is just for you. Be honest, be open, and let yourself dream again. You'd be amazed what dreams still live in your heart and your soul that are MEANT to become reality. If no one is there to tell you no or stand in your way, just imagine what you could accomplish.

What would you do if you knew you could achieve those dreams? What if it wasn't impossible or ridiculous? What would you do if you were guaranteed success if you just showed up and tried?

Reflect Exercise

I know the reflection and the work will be excruciatingly challenging, at times, because in order to make change, we need to see and feel deeper and intentionally.

Stay in the uncomfortable moments because that means something internally life changing is about to evolve. Embrace the fear because on the other side a lighter, true, happy, authentic, and strong version of yourself is standing. Every time one of these exercises begins I will be reminding you it's your time to GLOW. So without further ado...It's

GLOW TIME!

HINT - you don't have to share this with anyone!

Think back to that beautiful child who was about three or four years old who dreamt of being a teacher, astronaut, basketball player or Disney princess.

Do you remember who you wanted to be and what you wanted to stand for—before other people and other opinions got in the way?

Write your story from that perspective—from your little three year old heart.

Go ahead - I'm giving you permission!

Dig Deep

In order to create meaningful change, we need to pause and reflect on the people, routines, and patterns that shape our day-to-day experiences. This is about understanding who and what surrounds you and deciding if they truly support and contribute to your growth, or if they are keeping you stagnant or holding you back.

This exercise will prepare you for the next step in your journey. I know it's a hard one, but I'm here with you every step of the way. Take your time, be honest with yourself, and remember: you have the strength to create the life you deserve.

First, reflect on the following questions:

- Do you feel the need to be needed by others?

- Are you comfortable being alone, or do you keep people in your life just to avoid loneliness, even if they're not right for you?

- Are you seeking approval from others—a parent, friend, partner, or colleague?

- Do you ever question whether you're worthy of living a fulfilling life with supportive people and meaningful experiences?

- Do you feel as though good things, good people, and happiness are meant for others but not for you?

Here's the truth: you are worthy. You are worthy of love, joy, and fulfillment. You deserve a career that excites you, relationships that nourish you, and people who not only lean on you but also offer a shoulder to lean on when you need it.

Now, consider the people in your life:

- Who is in your life, and what purpose do they serve?

- Why did you choose them—or why did they choose you?

After reflecting on the questions above, consider: who truly deserves a place in your life—and who doesn't?

Next examine your routines:

- What are your routines, and why do you follow them?

- Are they helping you, or have they simply become comfortable?

- Are you holding onto certain habits because they feel familiar, even if they're not the best for you?

These are important, sometimes uncomfortable questions, but they lead to a deeper understanding of how you may be settling in your relationships, career, or personal life.

Oftentimes in life we settle a lot. We settle for people who not only are not good for us, but who cause a lot of pain. We settle in unfulfilling careers that don't excite or challenge us. It can be hard to see these things without deep reflection.

Take a moment to reflect:

- Where might you be settling in your life?

- Are you settling in your relationships? In your career? Why?

- Is there a history behind this—something that makes you doubt your worthiness or prevents you from asking for more?

This is a hard lesson, I know, because it challenges you to examine what—and who—you allow into your life. Sometimes, we hold onto people or routines that weigh us down, dim our light, or keep us from growing. It might be due to their jealousy, selfishness, or a dynamic that no longer works for you. These realizations can be painful, but they're crucial for change.

The good news is this: you have the power to choose differently. You have control over who and what stays in your life. You deserve to be surrounded by love, respect, and support, and to create a life that aligns with the best version of you.

Breaking Down Walls

Let's talk about the "walls" we have up—these walls are defense mechanisms you've developed along the way to protect yourself from pain, from being hurt again, and again. These walls usually come from past pain: maybe you experienced a trauma, had your heart broken, or felt judged or dismissed by peers, authority figures, your parents or even yourself. But here's the hard truth: while walls might shield you from the bad, they also block out the good—the possibilities and growth.

Think of these walls as barriers to your growth. They may seem protective, but in reality, they stop you from becoming the best version of yourself. Imagine a moat around a castle. Sure, it keeps out intruders and enemies, but it also prevents anything good—like love, connection, or support—from reaching you.

You might think you're just protecting yourself, but in the process, you might be missing out on meaningful opportunities and relationships. And let's not forget—others miss out on experiencing you, too.

The key isn't to eliminate walls entirely but to create healthy boundaries instead. Boundaries allow you to protect yourself while still remaining open to what nurtures and uplifts you. Learning to lower those walls—and deciding who is safe to let in—requires practice, reflection, and, most importantly, confidence.

Creating Healthy Boundaries

Imagine boundaries like different types of fences. Some people have no fence at all—they are completely vulnerable and exposed to the elements, but are also able to experience the unrestricted view of the day and are visited by beautiful creatures. They are completely open, vulnerable, and exposed to everything around them. While this means they can fully experience the beauty of connection, they are also at the mercy of harsh elements, uninvited guests, and unpredictable circumstances. Without protection, they may find themselves overwhelmed, drained, or taken advantage of.

Some have "pretend fences"—they look like they divide the property but other than that don't really serve a purpose. These are plastic fences—thin, flimsy, and mostly for show. They create the illusion of separation, but in reality, they don't do much. People can easily step over them or push through, disregarding the boundary entirely. Those with plastic fences may try to set limits, but they struggle to enforce them, often bending their own rules to accommodate others.

A wire fence offers more structure. It provides a clear boundary while still allowing visibility and airflow. It says, "I am here, and I have limits," but also, "I am open to connection in a way that feels safe for me." This is what healthy boundaries look like—strong enough to provide protection, yet flexible enough to allow relationships to thrive.

And then there are walls—thick, solid, and impossible to see through. These are built out of necessity, often after pain, betrayal, or exhaustion. Walls keep out the bad, but they also keep out the good. No one can hurt you, but no one can truly know you either. While they may have once been essential for survival, over time, they can become isolating, preventing growth and meaningful connection.

Here's the truth: walls that once protected you might now be holding you back. They can keep you stuck, preventing growth and deeper connections. By learning how to set clear, healthy limits with people and situations, you can start to dismantle these barriers. The goal isn't to tear them down overnight, but to slowly replace them with the kind of boundaries that keep you safe while allowing you to live, love, and connect. So, what kind of fence do you have? And is it time to build something new?

This work takes time and courage, but it's worth it. When you lower your walls, you make space for the love, opportunities, and growth you deserve. You create a life where you feel safe and connected—a life where you no longer stand in your own way. It's time to let go of what's holding you back while learning to have boundaries built on respect and not fear, on strength and not weakness.

Fear vs. Change

One of the most universal things I see in people is fear. Fear of making a change. Fear of taking a risk. Fear of stepping into the unknown. And honestly, it's completely normal—our brains are wired to keep us safe, and the unknown often feels like the opposite of safety. But here's the thing: living in fear means we stay stuck, and staying stuck often creates an even bigger risk—losing the chance to grow, to evolve, or to experience something extraordinary.

One of my favorite sayings is, "It's better to have loved and lost than never to have loved at all." I know that phrase stirs up a lot of mixed opinions, and that's fine. But for me, it speaks to a deep truth: I'd rather take a chance and know what something feels like—even if it doesn't work out—than to live my life wondering what if. The "what if" is so much heavier, so much harder to carry, than any failure ever could be.

Here's why: when we try and fail, we gain clarity. We learn. We grow. But when we don't try at all, we're left with endless questions and self-doubt. Regret is the heaviest burden to carry. And that's why I'm so passionate about encouraging you to take those risks, to push through the fear, and to embrace change.

Let's talk about change for a moment. I know it's scary. It's uncomfortable. It feels like standing on the edge of a cliff and not knowing if the parachute will open. But here's the truth: change is essential. It's not just important for personal growth—it's necessary for survival. Psychologists often refer to the concept of adaptive resilience, the ability to adjust to new circumstances and thrive in the face of challenges. Without change, we don't just stay stagnant; we start to wither.

Think about it like this: when babies are born, they can't walk or talk. They have to learn, step by step—first how to crawl, then how to stand, then how to walk, and eventually how to run. What if a baby decided, "You know what? Crawling is fine. I'm too scared to try anything else." That would be heartbreaking, right? We wouldn't be able to witness their full potential. The same is true for all of us, no matter our age or stage of life.

Fear of change isn't a flaw; it's human. But what separates those who thrive from those who don't is the willingness to feel the fear and make the leap anyway. Change is how we grow, how we find joy, and how we discover what's truly possible.

I'll leave you with this thought: everything in life happens for a reason. Every person, every challenge, every opportunity—it's all part of a greater plan. But you have a choice: will you embrace what's in front of you, or will you let fear hold you back? Life doesn't wait. So go out there. Take the risk. Make the change. Because the only thing worse than failing is never trying at all.

Now let's take a moment to dive deeper into this. The next exercise is designed to help you reflect on your own fears, your relationship with change, and what's holding you back. You're here because you're ready to do the work—and I'm here to help you every step of the way.

Are You Your Own Worst Enemy?

Alright, let's get real for a second. Have you ever stopped to think, "Wait, could I actually be the one standing in my own way?" I know, it's not the easiest thing to admit—but it's so common. We spend so much time worrying about keeping bad vibes, toxic people, or bad decisions out of our lives, but rarely do we look in the mirror and ask, "Am I the problem here?"

Here's what I mean. Sometimes, without even realizing it, we're the ones throwing up roadblocks to our own happiness and success. Maybe it's that you're too scared to go for that promotion, so you convince yourself it's "not the right time." Or you avoid trying something new—whether it's taking a different route to work, saying yes to an opportunity, or speaking up in a meeting—because, what if it doesn't work out?

Sound familiar? It's not just fear that's the issue here. Every time we let these small choices pile up, we're keeping ourselves stuck. We're saying no to growth; no to becoming the next-level version of ourselves; no to a life that feels bigger, bolder, and brighter. And that's not what you're here for, right?

Here's the thing: when you stop yourself from trying, when you stay comfy in that little bubble of "what I already know," you're not protecting yourself—you're limiting yourself. Sure, it feels safer in the moment, but over time, it chips away at your confidence, your joy, and your ability to create a life you love.

So here's the challenge: find one tiny way—just one—to stop getting in your own way today. Think small. Maybe it's finally sending that email you've been overthinking. Maybe it's trying something you've secretly wanted to do but have been too nervous to try. Or maybe it's as simple as catching yourself the next time your inner critic pipes up saying, "Nope, not today."

When you stop treating yourself like an enemy and start acting like your own best friend, everything shifts. You stop talking yourself out of things and start cheering yourself on. You stop seeing risks as scary and start seeing them as stepping stones. You stop staying small and start living large.

So go ahead—take that first step. I'll be here cheering you on every step of the way.

You in? Let's do this.

Masks

Every day, many of us navigate the world presenting an image that doesn't fully reflect who we truly are or what we feel inside. We put on a mask—a carefully constructed façade designed to hide our pain, shield our vulnerabilities, and project an image that we think the world will accept. These masks may help us feel safe, but they often come at a cost, and they most definitely take a toll.

I want you to think about the masks you wear. What do you show the world that doesn't match how you truly feel inside? Maybe you're the one who always seems "tough" or "put together," even though there's a whirlwind of emotions just beneath the surface. Maybe you play the role of the peacemaker, even when resentment or frustration simmers beneath. These masks can take on many forms, but they all serve a similar purpose: to protect you from judgment, rejection, or the fear of being seen too deeply.

I've met people from all walks of life—supermodels who feel unattractive, bodybuilders who don't believe they're strong enough, and intellectuals who doubt their intelligence. From the outside, these individuals seem to embody confidence, strength, or success, yet they carry insecurities and doubts, hidden behind their masks. Can you relate?

Now, I want you to take a step back and truly examine the mask you wear. Visualize it in your mind. What does it look like? How does it feel to put it on each day? What emotions or truths are you concealing behind it? Is it anger that you don't want others to see? Fear that feels too overwhelming to share? Disappointment or insecurity that you believe would make you appear weak?

As you reflect on your mask, I want you to take a moment to consider what lies beneath it. Underneath the mask is the real you—the version of yourself that is raw, vulnerable, and undeniably human. This version of you doesn't need to be perfect, because perfection isn't the goal. Authenticity is. And while it may feel safer to hide behind the mask, it's also isolating. The mask creates distance—between you and the people who care about you, and even between you and your own happiness.

Here's the hard truth: masks serve a purpose, but they aren't permanent. They come at a price: the price of losing sight of the true real genuine beautiful loveable only YOU. They aren't meant to define you. And as beautiful or necessary as the mask may seem, it will never compare to the beauty of the person behind it. You. The mask is not who you are—it's who you think you need to be, to be loved, accepted, to be.

Removing your mask isn't easy. It is scary as hell. It requires bravery, self-compassion, and a willingness to face the emotions you've worked so hard to hide. It will most definitely feel scary at first, because the mask has been a part of you for so long. But I promise you, beneath that mask is someone worth knowing. Beneath that mask is someone who deserves to feel seen, loved, and accepted for exactly who they are.

As you move forward in this journal, I encourage you to approach this process with curiosity and grace. You may uncover truths that are difficult to face. You may feel vulnerable or even exposed at times. But remember, this is a safe space for you to explore, reflect, and grow. I'm here with you every step of the way, and I'm honored to be part of your journey.

The next exercise will guide you in examining the masks you wear, the emotions they're hiding, and the reasons they exist. Together, we'll take the first steps toward uncovering the authentic you—the you who is capable of living a life of freedom, joy, and genuine connection.

Mask Exercise

This process may feel challenging, but it is also transformative. To move forward, we must first look inward. Take some time to reflect on the masks you wear in your daily life. What emotions are you hiding—anger, fear, insecurity, self-doubt? Why do you feel the need to wear these masks? Write openly and honestly. Remember, this is for you and only you. Let this be the first step in reclaiming the beauty of your authentic self.

I know the reflection and the work will be excruciatingly challenging, at times, because in order to make change, we need to see and feel deeper and intentionally.

Most of us don't really display to the world how we feel on a daily basis. We hide behind masks that cover up anger, disappointment, fear, insecurity, lack of self esteem, and more. It's

GLOW TIME!

What mask do you wear on a daily basis?

What feelings do you display ON your mask (what are you pretending to feel?—happy, content, etc.)?

What feelings are behind the mask—what are you really feeling (ex. sad, angry, frustrated)?

Where do you wear your masks? (ex. at work, at home, with friends, with your partner, etc.)

Why do you wear your mask? What purpose does it serve?

What changes can you make to live more authentically and be yourself without wearing the mask?

What changes from above can you start implementing today?

Consider the beauty that lies beneath that mask. In order to reveal that beauty, you are going to need to face the reasons why you wear the mask. All that mask is doing is keeping you from being your authentic self. You can do this!

Purge

You've been reflecting on your life, examining who's in it and what you want for yourself. Now it's time to look deeper. To move forward, you need to create space—space for growth, for clarity, and for the things and people that truly align with your values.

This next step is about letting go.

I know that can sound uncomfortable, maybe even harsh. There's a stigma around the idea of removing people or things from our lives, as if it's unkind or selfish. But I'm not asking you to be mean; I'm asking you to be kind—to yourself.

Picture your life as a tray, like the kind a server carries in a restaurant. That tray holds everything you juggle: relationships, obligations, work, dreams. If your tray is too full, there's no room left for you. It's time to assess what's taking up space in a way that drains you, and start letting those things—or people—go.

Think about the relationships in your life: colleagues, acquaintances, friends, even family or significant others. Who truly shows up for you? Who accepts you as you are? Who protects your energy and values your presence? Now think about the others—the ones who take more than they give, who don't appreciate you, who leave you feeling depleted.

Letting go isn't about confrontation or drama. It's not about blocking phone numbers or cutting ties in anger. It's about recognizing your worth and making space for relationships that uplift and sustain you. It's about shifting your focus to those who genuinely care for you and limiting the time, energy, and emotional investment you give to those who don't.

I want you to imagine your life as a dinner table. Who do you want at that table? Who do you trust to sit beside you in hard times? Who has proven, time and again, that they are truly there for you? Those are the people who belong.

If someone doesn't appreciate you, takes advantage of your kindness, or diminishes your value, it's time to reconsider their place in your life. By holding onto people or things that drain you, you're devaluing yourself—and you deserve better.

So here's your task: make a list of anyone or anything in your life that feels toxic, unhealthy, or unaligned with the person you're becoming. Be honest. Then, start considering ways to create distance or redefine those relationships.

This isn't about punishment. It's about prioritizing you.

Purge Exercise

I know the reflection and the work will be excruciatingly challenging, at times, because in order to make change, we need to see and feel deeper and intentionally. It's time to look at what you can and should let go of in your life—so that you can fill your plate with people and pursuits that serve you (not drain you!) It's

GLOW TIME!

WHAT in your life doesn't serve you?

WHO in your life doesn't serve you?

If these things or people don't bring anything positive to your life (and especially if they only bring negative to your life), why do you keep them around?

Who do you trust? Who is by your side during tough times?

How can you make room in your life for these healthy & supportive people?

Only invite those to your dinner table who truly have your back.

Compromise vs. Sacrifice

I want to talk about something that comes up often in conversations about relationships: the difference between compromise and sacrifice. This distinction is crucial because it affects how we navigate connections in every area of life—whether it's with friends, family, partners, or colleagues.

Compromise is about finding a way forward together. It happens when two people approach a disagreement or difference of opinion and work toward a solution that respects both sides. It's about balance—both people giving a little and getting a little in return. When you compromise, you're saying, "I see you, and I value this relationship enough to find common ground."

Sacrifice, though, is something entirely different. Sacrifice asks you to give up a part of yourself—your values, your needs, or even your identity—for the sake of someone else. Unlike compromise, it's not a shared effort. It can feel one-sided, and over time, it can take a toll.

Here's why this distinction matters so much: when you sacrifice too much of who you are in a relationship, you're chipping away at your authenticity. You may find yourself saying "yes" when you want to say "no," agreeing to things that don't align with your values, or suppressing your needs to keep the peace. And while it might seem like you're helping the relationship by doing this, it often leads to frustration, bitterness, or resentment—because you're not being true to yourself.

Let me be clear: compromise strengthens relationships. It's about building bridges and working together. Sacrifice, on the other hand, weakens relationships by asking you to lose sight of who you are.

It's not about refusing to bend or insisting on getting your way. It's about protecting the parts of you that matter most—your values, your boundaries, and the core of who you are. These are the things that make you you, and the healthiest relationships are the ones that honor and celebrate that.

If you find yourself constantly sacrificing—giving up your happiness, your peace, or your identity—pause and reflect. Ask yourself: Am I compromising, or am I sacrificing? Compromise feels like collaboration; sacrifice feels like a loss.

Here's the truth: no relationship worth keeping will ask you to give up the most important parts of yourself to maintain it. Compromise builds connection, but sacrifice, when it comes at the expense of your identity, can erode it.

So remember this: protect your boundaries. Hold onto your values. Be open to compromise, but never let someone take so much that you're left feeling less than whole. You deserve relationships that support you as you are—not ones that ask you to shrink to fit.

Trust me on this—you'll thank yourself for honoring who you are.

The Lighthouse Beacon

Do you sometimes wonder why you have certain people in your life that seem to take more than they contribute? Does it almost feel like you're attracting them? Well, I don't know how to gently say this but, there's a pretty good chance that you are. I'm not saying you're a bad person—that you're broken or that you deserve to attract unhealthy, unstable, toxic, emotionally unavailable individuals. I'm saying I believe that due to our past relationships, experiences, and even our personalities (which may be absolutely beautiful, genuine and loving) we become magnets to people that are not good for us. But don't worry, I'm going to explain how I believe this happens, and what you can do to change this pattern in your life.

Imagine a lighthouse. Its role is not only to warn boats that there is land nearby they could crash into, but also a safe haven leading boats safely to land—a beacon of hope in the dark.

What if I told you that sometimes the energy or vibe we give off also attracts the wrong people just like a lighthouse. Then we unintentionally become magnets drawing in everything we DON'T want. Follow me for a second.

Let's say you are trustworthy, dependable, loving, nurturing and forgiving. While that may sound like a dream come true to you, that may also sound like a dream come true for an unhealthy person who then misinterprets that "light" as a message that says, "you won't have to earn my trust, you automatically have it. You can always depend on me…I will always be there for you. I WANT to take care of you, and I will. It's ok if you make mistakes because I will forgive you…over and over again."

Now, while that may not be your intention at all, good people seem to have an uncanny ability to attract unhealthy individuals. Your lighthouse calls in people like you, but also people that feed off of—and need—people like you.

Think about the people who you know take advantage of you. Do they meet any of the examples I just explained? Could you have inadvertently let your lighthouse call them in by their interpretation of your bright light?

Now the question is, what to do about it. No, you don't have to change who YOU are. You don't have to sacrifice the gentle, genuine, loving, caring, trustworthy, dependable, loving, nurturing and forgiving parts of you that make you, you.

What you have to start doing is fine-tuning that light. How can you be true to yourself without attracting those ill-intended individuals who will suck you dry?

The first step is awareness. That's all.

The second step is realizing what message your beacon is giving out. How can you maintain the integrity of who you are at your core without becoming a doormat? How can you tweak that signal/light/beacon to also emit other messages? Messages that say, "I am strong, I am loving, I am nurturing but I have healthy boundaries," "I am trustworthy but I will not be taken advantage of" or "I'm forgiving but there's only so many chances you get. I will not be your toy."

The third step is building confidence in who you are and what you have to offer.

The fourth step is establishing and maintaining healthy boundaries.

The fifth step is sticking to the promise you make to yourself to be respected, and honored as much as you respect and honor those in your life.

The final step is letting go of people, habits, patterns, circumstances, commitments, roles and individuals that don't respect and honor you.

Spring Cleaning

This week is all about spring cleaning, and I couldn't be more excited for you. By now, you've taken time to reflect on what you want from your life—what truly matters to you. You've made your list, started the process of purging, and now it's time to go deeper. This week is intentionally designed to help you clear away the clutter—not just the physical or relational, but from your entire life.

Take this opportunity to reflect, review, and assess. Revisit your notes, your handouts, and your worksheets. Make sure they're complete, and spend time reading through them. Read them again and again, if needed. Think critically about the changes you need to make for the fresh start you deserve.

Over the past lessons, we've carefully examined your life. We've explored what's been holding you back, what's unhealthy, and what no longer serves you. You've also identified what you wish you had and what's worth building toward. Now, it's time to move forward with intention.

There's a phrase in Latin, tabula rasa, meaning "clean slate." That's the mindset I want you to embrace as we wrap up this process. Give yourself permission to clear out everything that doesn't align with the life you want to create—people, habits, beliefs, commitments. Nothing is off-limits.

It's possible to start fresh, I promise you. Your past does not define you. You are capable of shaping your life into one that feels fulfilling and authentic. But remember, this takes effort, honesty, and courage. Do the work.

Take this week to commit fully to your spring cleaning.

Communication

One of the most common issues I see in my work—whether it's with couples, friends, or coworkers—is communication. More specifically, it's how we approach conflict in a way that either strengthens the relationship or chips away at it. One tool that I consistently come back to with clients is the use of "I" statements. It's simple, effective, and rooted in some solid psychological principles for managing emotions and reducing conflict.

Let's start with the basics. When you're upset, it's easy to fall into what we call the blame game. You feel hurt or frustrated, and your instinct might be to say something like, "You never listen!" "You always make us late!" While it's natural to want to call out the other person, this approach rarely gets the results you're looking for. Why? Because it puts the other person on the defensive. When someone feels attacked, their first reaction is usually to protect themselves—not to hear you out or try to understand your feelings.

This is where "I" statements come in. Instead of focusing on what the other person did wrong, you focus on how you feel and what you need. It might sound like a small tweak, but it can completely change the tone of a conversation.

For example, let's say your partner was driving too fast, missed a turn, and now you're late for dinner. You might feel tempted to say something like, "You're always rushing! You never think about how stressful this is for me!" But that kind of statement often just escalates the situation.

An "I" statement shifts the focus: "I feel really stressed when we're running late for a reservation. It makes me anxious, and I'd prefer if we could plan to leave a little earlier next time."

Notice how this changes the conversation? Instead of blaming, you're sharing how the situation impacts you. This approach not only helps keep the conversation calmer but also increases the chances of the other person actually hearing what you're saying.

Here's the catch: not every sentence that starts with "I" is an "I" statement. For instance, "I hate that you're always late" isn't helpful because it's still about them, not you. A true "I" statement focuses on your feelings and needs without passing judgment.

What's great about "I" statements is how versatile they are. They're not just for romantic relationships. You can use them with friends, family, and coworkers. They're especially helpful in professional situations where staying respectful and emotionally neutral is key.

Psychologically, "I" statements tap into what's known as emotional intelligence—the ability to recognize, understand, and express your emotions in a way that doesn't harm the relationship. It's also a way to maintain healthy boundaries by focusing on what's within your control: your own emotions and how you communicate them.

The goal here isn't to win an argument but to foster understanding and connection. "I" statements make it easier to do that because they take the blame out of the equation and invite collaboration instead.

Now it's your turn to try this out. In the next exercise, you'll get a chance to practice crafting "I" statements and see how they can shift the tone of even the toughest conversations.

Communication Exercise

Think of the last time you had an argument with your partner or coworker. Replay the conversation. Now, rewrite the conversation using the "I" statement guidelines: focus on how you feel and what you need.

Think of a recent time you felt frustrated with a friend, family member, or child. See if you can reframe the way you communicate that frustration through "I" statements. "I feel…" and "I need…"

Be True to Yourself

Let's begin with a fundamental truth: being true to yourself is the cornerstone of living a fulfilled, meaningful life. This might sound simple, but in practice, it's one of the hardest things we'll ever do. Why? Because it requires us to quiet the noise of the outside world—the expectations, the opinions, the "shoulds"—and tune in to the voice within that knows what we need, want, and value most.

Psychologically, this process is called self-actualization—a concept introduced by Abraham Maslow in his hierarchy of needs. Self-actualization is about reaching our fullest potential by living in alignment with our true selves. It's not just about achieving goals or checking off accomplishments; it's about becoming who we were always meant to be. And that starts with understanding who we are at our core.

But here's the thing: many of us have spent so much time adapting to others' expectations that we've lost touch with our inner compass. Maybe you've been told to follow a certain path because it's "safe" or "practical." Maybe you've pushed your own needs aside to prioritize others, believing that self-sacrifice is the only way to show love. Over time, this disconnect can leave us feeling stuck, unfulfilled, or even lost.

So how do we reconnect with ourselves? How do we uncover what truly matters to us?

It begins with self-reflection. Take a moment to pause and ask yourself some big, life-defining questions:

- What do I truly want? Not what I think I should want, but what I genuinely desire.

- What brings me joy? Not fleeting happiness, but deep, soul-level fulfillment.

- What am I afraid to admit I want? Fear often hides the truth, but it's also a doorway to discovery.

This isn't just a theoretical exercise—it's a practice grounded in psychological research. Studies on self-determination theory show that when we live in alignment with our intrinsic goals (what we deeply value), we experience greater well-being, motivation, and resilience. In contrast, pursuing extrinsic goals—like seeking validation or approval—can leave us feeling empty, even if we appear successful on the surface.

Now, imagine your life if you leaned fully into your truth. Picture it vividly:

- What does your day-to-day look like?
- Who are you spending your time with?

- What are you doing that makes you feel alive, inspired, and proud?

- How does it feel in your body to live a life aligned with your deepest values?

Visualization is a powerful tool. Research in neuropsychology shows that when we vividly imagine a desired future, our brain begins to create pathways to make it a reality. It's like planting a seed in your mind that, with time and care, will grow into something extraordinary.

But here's the challenge: being true to yourself isn't always easy. It requires courage to confront uncomfortable truths, to let go of habits or relationships that no longer serve you, and to move toward the unknown. It also means giving yourself permission to evolve, knowing that your needs and desires may change over time—and that's okay.

As you navigate this process, remember that being true to yourself doesn't mean you have to have all the answers right now. It's about being curious, open, and willing to explore. It's about tuning into your inner voice and honoring it, even when it whispers instead of shouts.

Be TRUE to Yourself Exercise

This exercise is about creating clarity. Clarity isn't just about knowing what you want; it's about understanding why it matters to you. And this clarity is the foundation for change.

1. Reflect on Your Wants and Needs

Write down the things you want most in your life. Don't censor yourself. Let it flow, even if it feels big, scary, or unrealistic. Then, dig deeper:

- Why do I want this?

- How does it align with my values?

- What fears or doubts come up when I think about pursuing this?

2. Visualize Your Ideal Life

Close your eyes and imagine your dream life in detail. What do you see, hear, and feel? Who are you in this vision? Write it all down as if you're journaling from the future, living that life.

3. Identify One Actionable Step

Change happens one step at a time. What's one, small meaningful action you can take today to move closer to the life you want? It doesn't have to be monumental—just intentional.

Remember: the journey to being true to yourself is ongoing. It's not about perfection or achieving a fixed destination. It's about living authentically, with intention and courage. The more you honor your truth, the more aligned and fulfilling your life will become.

This work isn't easy, but it's worth it. And the most beautiful part? You already have everything you need within you to begin.

I know the reflection and the work will be excruciatingly challenging, at times, because in order to make change, we need to see and feel deeper and intentionally.

The only person who knows how you can be true to yourself is YOU. I can't do that for you (my magic wand is in the shop). It's

GLOW TIME!

What do you want your dream life to look like? (describe it in detail)

How would it feel to live THAT life that you just described?

To get to a place where you love your life, you need to know what that looks like. So dream away!!

Be KIND to Yourself

Let's talk about self-kindness. I know—it sounds simple, right? But if you're anything like most of us, it's probably one of the hardest things to practice.

Consider this: When did you learn to be so hard on yourself? Believe it or not, that inner critic of yours—it wasn't there when you were born. You didn't come into this world judging yourself for every little thing. That voice was learned—picked up along the way through life experiences, social expectations, and maybe even well-meaning people who thought criticism was the same as love.

Enter cognitive-behavioral theory, a cornerstone in psychology that's all about how our thoughts shape our emotions and actions. According to this approach, the way you talk to yourself — your inner dialogue — directly impacts how you feel and what you do. So, if you're constantly criticizing yourself, you're feeding a cycle of negativity that makes it harder to grow, thrive, or just feel good about who you are.

But here's the good news: just like that inner critic was learned, it can also be unlearned. The first step is awareness. Start paying attention to the stories you're telling yourself. Are they rooted in truth, or are they old narratives you've outgrown? Most of the time, that harsh voice is just fear dressed up as "motivation." But fear isn't a sustainable motivator. Encouragement is.

Think of it this way: if a friend came to you feeling defeated, would you say, "Well, maybe you're just not good enough?" Of course not! You'd probably tell them, "You're doing your best, and that's enough." So, why don't we extend that same kindness to ourselves?

Here's where I want you to really focus on: replacing criticism with curiosity. Psychologist Carol Dweck's research on the growth mindset teaches us that instead of seeing mistakes as failures, we can reframe them as opportunities to learn. Instead of, "I'm so bad at this," you could try, "What can I learn from this?" Instead of, "I'll never figure it out," ask, "What's one small step I can take to make this easier?"

Notice how those shifts feel in your body. One opens up possibilities. The other shuts them down.

And let's talk about one more thing: perfection. Spoiler alert—it doesn't exist. What does exist is progress. And progress happens when you give yourself room to breathe, space to stumble, and permission to just be human.

When you stop worrying about other people's opinions and start tuning into your own voice, you create freedom—freedom to show up authentically, to make bold moves, and to live without constantly second-guessing yourself.

Here's what I want you to remember:

1. Catch the critic. Start noticing when you're being hard on yourself. Awareness is everything.

2. Pause and reframe. Ask yourself, "What would I say to a friend in this situation?" Then say that to yourself.

3. Celebrate the small wins. Progress, not perfection, is the goal. Every step forward counts.

Self-kindness isn't about being lazy or letting yourself off the hook. It's about creating the emotional safety you need to grow, thrive, and tackle life's challenges with courage.

You deserve grace. You deserve space. You deserve kindness. Not because of what you achieve or how you perform, but because you're human—and that's enough.

Now, let's keep working on this together. It's a process, not a destination. And trust me, you're already further along than you think.

Be KIND to Yourself Exercise

I know the reflection and the work will be excruciatingly challenging, at times, because in order to make change. we need to see and feel deeper and intentionally.

We are our harshest critics. We live in a world full of judgment - even if it's unintentional. It's

GLOW TIME!

What are some people's or society's perceptions of you that may feel negative or heavy?

That negative self-talk has to change.

For every negative thing you say to yourself or you hear, write it down in the left column. In the right column, write something positive to flip it around:

What positive traits above stood out for you? Any surprise you?

What are some of your own positive opinions of yourself? The ones that make you a better person? (Do you love your smile? Were you super smart in school? Can you whistle really well?)

How can you focus on these positive traits & attributes?

When you free yourself from others' negative opinions, you become free. Be sure to give yourself some grace as you transition into this freedom.

Self-Care

Let's talk about self-care. When I bring this up with people, I usually get one of two reactions: "What is that?" or "I don't have time for that." Sound familiar?

Here's the thing: self-care is simply taking the time to take care of yourself. But while it sounds simple, it's not always easy. Life happens. Work, family, stress, money—everything pulls at you, demanding your attention. And somewhere in the mix, you get lost.

But here's the truth: self-care is not a luxury. It's a necessity. It's deeply personal, which means there's no one-size-fits-all formula. What works for someone else might not work for you, and that's okay.

If you're sitting here thinking, "I don't even know where to start," that's your first sign that self-care has probably been pushed to the back burner for too long.

Now, I get it. You're busy. You probably have a packed schedule. But I bet you still find time to brush your teeth or take a shower (I hope!). Those little routines are non-negotiable, right? Self-care deserves to be treated the same way—like something essential you build into your life.

Here's where most people get stuck: they think self-care has to be this huge production, like a spa day or a week-long retreat. It doesn't. Self-care can be anything that makes you feel good, centered, and recharged. Maybe that's hitting the gym, dancing like nobody's watching, taking a long walk, or even trying something new and adventurous like bungee jumping (if that's your thing). It could also be as simple as sitting in your car for five minutes with no interruptions. The point is, it has to be something you genuinely enjoy.

Start small. Maybe it's just five minutes a week. Eventually, you can work up to five minutes a day. Then 30 minutes. Then—who knows?—maybe even an hour. But here's the catch: if you don't plan it, it won't happen. Self-care requires intentionality.

And let me say this loud and clear, especially for the moms reading this: taking care of yourself is not selfish. I know it can feel that way when your world revolves around your kids, your spouse, your job, or anyone else who depends on you. But let me ask you this—how can you show up for them if you're running on empty?

Here's the truth: when you're rested, healthy, and fulfilled, you're better for everyone around you. You're a better mom, partner, friend, sibling, coworker—everything. It's like that saying about putting your oxygen mask on first. You can't pour from an empty cup.

So, I'm giving you permission (not that you need it!) to make self-care a priority. Schedule that date night. Take that vacation. Call the friend who makes you laugh until your cheeks hurt. Do whatever refills your tank, because you're worth it.

You deserve to feel good. You've earned it. And the best part? The people in your life will benefit from the happier, healthier version of you.

Make the time. Start now. You're worth every second.

Overcoming Your Biggest Fears

I have a good friend who, by chance and circumstance, has become one of my very best friends and closest confidants. Here's a recent exchange we had.

Friend: Why can't I do anything?

Me: What do you mean?

Friend: I'm not telling you to give me direction, I'd love to create something, I have no motivation.

Me: Do you want the truth?

Friend: It's like a block, Like what the hell would I do? Sure, truth.

Me: You care TOO much about what the fuck people think, I don't give a fuck, like I care, but not enough that I won't make an ass out of myself while I get it done.

Friend: Do I care what people think or am I too critical of myself?

Me: Your fear is what people will think. My fear is regretting not making it happen, even if it's a hot mess —not that I want it to be.

Friend: I don't even have an idea.

Me: I'd rather try and it suck and be disappointed and then learn from my mistakes and try again.

Friend: There's nothing I'm even passionate about.

Me: I have a million ideas of things you COULD do— so many gifts you have but you don't see them. You can't have passion if you're terrified of judgement.

Friend: Yeah, I don't.

Me: Passion supersedes giving a fuck. Like your doodles could be an adult coloring book. Someone friggin permanently scarred their skin in ink with one!"

Here's the truth. Your biggest fear is almost 99.9% in your head. Most often our greatest fears are rooted in caring way too much about what others think.

Overcoming Perfectionism

In my clinical training as a therapist, we were taught how to do what we do seamlessly. After all, people are coming to us, "the experts," for help because we "know it all" and "we know how to fix your problem."

I eventually realized that the therapeutic profession, while beautiful and well intentioned, only hindered my emotional growth because I had to "be perfect" for my patients. I had to look impeccably professional. Hair—check; makeup—check; perfect shade of blush silk shirt that's soft & airy—check; unwrinkled & dry cleaned—check; not see through—check; perfect black pencil skirt—check; past knee length—check; listen, respond, don't share personal life—check. Oh my God! Talk about pressure and so unrealistic!

Since my childhood, I've always strived and poured all of my energy to overachieve. And as a result, there has never ever been anything in my entire life that I wanted that I have not attained. I'm the overachiever of overachievers. I started second grade at five years old, graduated high school at 17 with honors, was on my own at 17 in college with a full tuition scholarship, graduated with honors from college while finishing a semester early, received a scholarship at my prestigious alma mater—the list goes on.

Everything had to be perfect. My grades had to be perfect. My assignments were completed before they were due (they were months early). There were even times in college that I resubmitted papers to my favorite English professor, who was real and raw and offered us the opportunity for constant feedback. There was a paper that I probably wrote, and resubmitted (poor woman), about 10 times (I'm not exaggerating).

I wanted that PERFECT grade, and the more I worked on it, the more my grade improved, until I decided that it was as good as I could possibly make it. And it was, I earned my A+.

It wasn't until this very moment, that I realized her strategy wasn't about perfection, her strategy was about progress and skill. The more I attempted to "perfect" the paper, the more I was learning. It was actually genius of her.

The message I want to relay to you, is that if you try to be perfect, which is completely impossible and unsustainable, you're never going to start.

In life, in entrepreneurship, in relationships, you're going to make mistakes. Things are going to get ugly. You're not going to look your best, you're not going to be smooth in your emails, you're not going to create the perfect online course the first time around, you're not going to always catch the typo in the post you made. You're going to reread and rewrite things and you're still going to make mistakes. It's called being human!

So, as you're reading this I can guarantee that there are at least 10 things in your life that you haven't even attempted because you're so scared you'll fail. You haven't started because you want to do it the RIGHT WAY...the PERFECT WAY. If you continue on this path, it's never going to get done.

I want you to repeat after me "PROGRESS NOT PERFECTION."

I want you to make this your new mantra. Say it to yourself all day, stand in front of the mirror, make it your new cellphone wallpaper, set an alarm, put a "post-it" on your bathroom mirror.

Ironically, I also remember another day at that same faithful university: there was a flyer inside of a bathroom stall in the dorms that said, "I know I'm not junk, because God made me, and he don't make no junk."

My point being is you're not perfect, you are "perfectly imperfect." You're going to make mistakes, you're going to fall, you're going to fail. The difference between someone who is successful and someone who fails, is resilience. It's what you do after you fall that makes all the difference in the world. So, I challenge you to take the leap in whatever it is that you haven't done because you're waiting to be perfect.

You know how I love my challenges, and I don't disappoint so I have one for you today.

I want you to make the most "perfectly imperfect" attempt at that effort. And whether you feel like you failed or you succeeded—without a doubt what you have done is GROWN! Just like that (wink).

Restructure Your Life

Here's where the fun part comes in: you get to design this plan your way. It doesn't need to be complicated. Forget perfection. Whether it's scribbled on a napkin, written in a beautiful planner, or jotted down with crayons on a piece of scrap paper—it doesn't matter. What matters is that you make it yours.

Start by thinking about the roadblocks that could show up. Life has a way of testing us, so ask yourself: What might try to pull me back into old habits? Maybe it's stress, certain people, or even your own inner critic. Whatever it is, name it. Then, for each potential obstacle, create an actionable step to address it. Not vague ideas—concrete actions. If stress derails you, maybe your plan includes a daily walk or journaling session. If saying "yes" to everyone else's demands is your Achilles' heel, your plan might involve practicing the word "no" or setting firm boundaries.

Pro tip: accountability is everything. Find someone who will cheer you on while keeping you honest. It could be a friend, colleague, or family member, but they need to be one of the supportive, healthy people you've intentionally kept in your circle. (Remember, this is not the job for someone you've already lovingly let go of in your spring cleaning process.) Share your plan with them and ask for their support.

Finally, anchor your plan in your daily life. Put it on your calendar. Schedule the gym time. Plan your meals. Block off dates for that dream vacation you've always talked about. If you're committing to drinking more water, track it. If you want to spend more time with loved ones, decide when and where you'll make that happen. Progress thrives in structure—it doesn't just "happen."

I know this might feel overwhelming, but here's the truth: this is where the magic happens. This is the part where you honor the work you've done by showing up for yourself in a way that's consistent and compassionate. This is the part where you love yourself enough to make these changes stick.

You've already proven how strong and capable you are by making it this far. And I couldn't be prouder. You are building a life that reflects your deepest values and dreams—a life you truly love.

Congratulations on all you've accomplished so far. Stay with it, because you're not just making changes; you're creating transformation. Let's keep going. There's more good stuff ahead, and I can't wait to see what you do next.

Creating Your Utopia

Let's talk about something that can change your life: your ideal world—your version of utopia. I know, "utopia" sounds like a big, unattainable dream, but bear with me. This isn't about creating a perfect, impossible fantasy. It's about giving yourself permission to imagine a life that feels deeply aligned with who you are and what you truly want.

Here's why this matters: when we don't know what we're working toward, life tends to feel overwhelming or directionless. It's like driving without a map—you're moving, but where are you going? Many of us spend years feeling stuck or unfulfilled, not because we're incapable, but because we've never taken the time to define what fulfilled actually looks like.

Psychologically, this is critical. Studies on goal-setting and visualization show that creating a clear vision of your desired future activates parts of your brain that help you move toward it. Neuroscience refers to this as the reticular activating system: a network in your brain that helps you notice opportunities, patterns, and connections aligned with your goals. In simpler terms, when you know what you want, your brain starts filtering the world to help you get there.

But here's the catch: a lot of people avoid this kind of deep reflection. Why? Because it can feel uncomfortable. What if you realize you've been living a life that doesn't match your values? What if you dream about things that feel too big or too far out of reach? That discomfort is real—but it's also where growth begins.

Now, let's walk through an exercise that I've used with so many clients over the years. It's simple, but powerful, and it starts with a question: what if a miracle happened tonight?

Imagine you go to sleep tonight, and while you're resting, something magical happens. When you wake up tomorrow, your life looks and feels exactly as you've always wanted it to. It's your ideal world—your personal utopia.

Let's break it down, moment by moment.

Where are you waking up? Is it in the house of your dreams, surrounded by nature, in a bustling city, or maybe somewhere completely new? What do you notice first—sunlight streaming through the window, the smell of freshly brewed coffee, or the sound of someone you love beside you?

What's your morning routine? Are you diving into meaningful work, savoring a slow breakfast, or heading out for an adventure? Who are you spending your day with? Are they energizing, supportive, and aligned with the person you want to be?

What does your career look like? Are you running a business you're passionate about? Traveling the world while working remotely? Maybe you're retired or pursuing creative projects. Whatever it is, imagine how it feels to spend your day doing something that truly lights you up.

As the day winds down, where are you? What's your environment like? Are you in a home you love, surrounded by family or friends, or enjoying the peaceful solitude you've always craved? And at the end of it all, when your head hits the pillow, what emotions are you holding onto—peace, pride, gratitude, fulfillment?

This exercise isn't just about daydreaming. It's about clarity. Without a clear vision, it's nearly impossible to make meaningful changes in your life. Think of it this way: if you don't know where you're going, how can you ever get there?

And let's be real—life doesn't always cooperate with our plans. There will be challenges, detours, and unexpected twists. But when you're grounded in a clear vision of what you want, those obstacles feel less daunting. You can adjust your path while keeping your destination in sight.

So, here's your challenge: take some time to sit with these questions and write down your answers. Be as detailed and honest as you can. Let yourself dream without limits, without judgment, and without the "what ifs" that hold you back. This is about you and what truly matters to you—not anyone else.

Clarity is the first step to transformation. By doing this exercise, you're giving yourself the gift of direction, purpose, and intention. And that's how you start building a life you love.

Take your time with this, and don't rush the process. This is about laying the foundation for something extraordinary—your future. I'll see you in the next section, ready to take the next step.

Maintaining Your Life

We've torn it all down—the old beliefs, the limiting patterns, and the roles that no longer served you. We've done the deep work of purging what held you back—old relationships, cluttered spaces, even the masks you wore to protect yourself. You've started rebuilding, step by step, imagining the life you want and taking action toward those changes.

At this point, I'm hoping, cheering, and wholeheartedly believing that you've started to see glimpses of what's possible. You've made progress, and that's incredible.But let's pause for a moment and talk about what happens next. Because here's the thing: change doesn't end when you take the first steps.

Transformation is a process, not an event. And to keep moving forward, you'll need to maintain the changes you've worked so hard to create. Why is that so important? Because, like it or not, our brains love patterns. The neural pathways in our mind—the ones that guide our habits and responses—have been carved over years of repetition. When life gets messy, stressful, or even just a little too familiar, those old patterns have a sneaky way of pulling us back. It's not because you're failing or doing something wrong; it's just how the brain works.

Here's where the real challenge lies: staying committed to your new path and the framework you've created to support the version of you that you're becoming.

Check in with yourself as you continue on your new path. Keep track of the obstacles that may creep in and try to derail your efforts. Remember: don't say "yes" when you mean "no." If you find yourself slipping back into unhealthy routines when life gets busy or stressful, notice that and revisit your restructuring plan and make a map to get back on track. Keep planning those meals, setting gym days, and scheduling time for rest and reflection.

Keep checking in with your accountability person. If you find yourself getting off track, they are a great person to reach out to. They will be able to reflect to you how far you have come and they will be able to encourage you along the way through the good times and the hard times.

I'm so proud of how far you've come. You've done the hard work of digging deep, and you've built something beautiful—something lasting. Keep going. I'm here, cheering you on every step of the way. You've got this.

Congratulations on creating a life you love. Let's keep that momentum going.

Maintaining Your Life Exercise

I know the reflection and the work has been excruciatingly challenging, at times, because in order to make change, we need to see and feel deeper and intentionally.

Now that you've made some important changes in your life, it's time to create a plan to maintain those changes. It's

GLOW TIME!

Whenever you feel stuck or pulled into an old pattern, revisit this part to help you stay on track.

Think about anything that will stand in the way of maintaining the changes you have made (or are working toward). Write them out. Map out how you can stay on track through these difficulties.

Who are your accountability partners? Make a list of at least three people and include specific ways you want them to help you.

Pull out your calendar. Schedule your time at the gym or other self-care activities. Schedule and buy tickets for that trip you've always wanted. Pencil in check-ins with your accountability partners.

This is the part where you love yourself enough to make the changes to make it stick!

Congratulations on creating a life you love!

www.ingramcontent.com/pod-product-compliance
Lightning Source LLC
Chambersburg PA
CBHW052032030426
42337CB00027B/4976